LOWRIDERS

by Lisa Bullard

⌐ Lerner Publications Company • Minneapolis

Special thanks to Pete Salas of Los Padrinos Lowriders Club of St. Paul for help with this book.

For Wendy, who always aims high!–LB

Text copyright © 2007 by Lerner Publications Company

Lerner Publications Company
A division of Lerner Publishing Group
241 First Avenue North
Minneapolis, MN 55401 U.S.A.

Website address: www.lernerbooks.com

Words in **bold** type are explained in a glossary on page 30.

Library of Congress Cataloging-in-Publication Data

Bullard, Lisa.
    Lowriders / by Lisa Bullard.
        p.   cm. — (Pull ahead books)
    Includes index.
    ISBN-13: 978-0-8225-6379-2 (lib. bdg. : alk. paper)
    ISBN-10: 0-8225-6379-7 (lib. bdg. : alk. paper)
    1. Lowriders—Juvenile literature. I. Title.
    TL255.2.B85 2007
    629.28'72—dc22   2006019111

Manufactured in the United States of America
1 2 3 4 5 6 — JR — 12 11 10 09 08 07

Have you ever seen a car dance?

Lowriders can dance. Some lowriders can hop!

All lowriders can drop low to the
ground. How do they do it?

Most lowriders use **hydraulics**.

The hydraulics are part of the car's suspension. The suspension connects the wheels to the car.

Pumps raise and lower the car. The pumps are in the trunk. These pumps are silver. Blue batteries power the pumps on this lowrider.

One switch makes the front go up or down. Another controls the back. Other switches control each wheel.

But why are lowriders built to go low?
Lowrider owners like to drive low and
slow. It gets people's attention.

Mexican Americans built the first lowriders.

Many lowriders also have fancy paint jobs. Owners use many coats of paint to get a shine!

12

Some lowriders also have pictures painted on them. These pictures are called murals.

Owners may add spotlights, badges, and sirens. These parts make their cars flashier.

Owners also add **chrome**. Chrome makes metal parts shine very brightly.

This lowrider has shiny wheels. It has small tires. They make the lowrider sit even lower.

Some owners work to make their lowriders special. This lowrider's doors open in a different direction.

Many decorate the inside of their
lowriders. This lowrider has lots of
soft velvet. It even has seats that
spin around.

Small, chain-link steering wheels are also popular. They are called "fat man" steering wheels. These small wheels give big guys plenty of room!

Some lowriders are loud and low.
That is because they have very large
sound systems.

Some lowriders even have strange things like fish tanks in them! Do you see the TV in this lowrider?

Many lowrider owners are members of lowrider clubs. They put the names of their clubs on special plaques, or signs.

Did you know that there are different kinds of lowriders? This lowrider is called a **bomb**. It is made from a very old car. This car is a 1949 Buick.

This lowrider is called a **traditional**. Traditionals are made from cars built in the 1960s and 1970s. This is a 1963 Chevrolet Impala.

Euros are lowriders made from cars built in Europe and Japan. This euro is a Volkswagen Beetle. Volkswagen cars are built in Germany.

But not all lowriders are cars. There are also lowrider trucks and motorcycles. This is a lowrider van.

There are even lowrider bicycles.
Maybe you can build one yourself.
Then you can ride low and slow too!

Facts about Lowriders

- The first lowriders were made by members of the Mexican-American community. Lowriding is still an important tradition for many Mexican Americans. But a love for lowriding has now spread as far as Japan.

- Owners have lowered their cars in different ways over the years. At first, owners put sandbags or other heavy things in the trunk.

- Other early lowriders used hydraulics from airplanes to make the cars go up and down.

- For lowrider shows, owners often put mirrors on the ground under their cars. Then everyone can see that even the bottoms of their lowriders are decorated!

Parts of a Lowrider

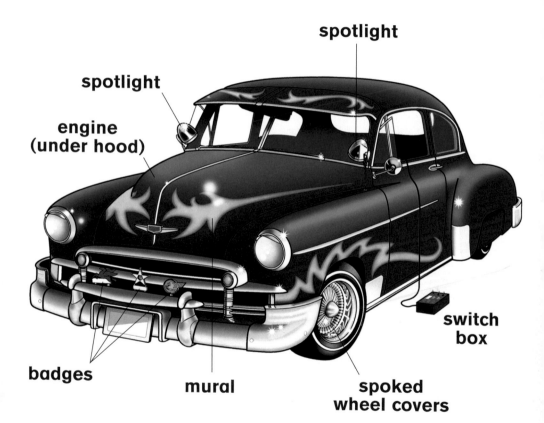

spotlight

spotlight

engine
(under hood)

switch
box

badges

mural

spoked
wheel covers

Glossary

bomb: the oldest kind of lowrider, built from cars that were made before 1959

chrome: silver-colored metal

Euros: lowriders made from cars from European or Japanese carmakers

hydraulics: a system that uses liquids like water or oil under pressure to move something

Mexican Americans: Americans whose families originally came to the United States from Mexico

sound systems: car stereos that play CDs or tapes

traditional: a lowrider that was made between 1959 and the mid-1970s

More about Lowriders

Check out these books and websites to learn more about lowrider cars and bikes.

Books

Maurer, Tracy. *Lowriders*. Vero Beach, FL: Rourke Publishing, 2004.

Soto, Gary. *My Little Car*. New York: Putnam's, 2006.

Websites

Lowrider Bikes: A Way of Life
http://www.azstarnet.com/public/packages/Wakefield/wake12.htm
Read about a group of Arizona kids and their amazing lowrider bikes.

Los Padrinos Lowriders Club: Club Members' Cars Page
http://lospadrinos.com
The Los Padrinos lowriders club is based in St. Paul, Minnesota. Check out the club's website to see some of the members' cool lowriders.

Index

Photo Acknowledgments

The photographs in this book are used the permission of: © Mike Key, front cover, pp. 3, 5, 6, 9, 10, 13, 15, 20, 23, 24, 25, 26; © Ted Soqui/CORBIS, pp. 4, 14, 17, 21; © Jeffrey Zuehlke, p. 7; © Todd Strand/Independent Picture Service, pp. 8, 16, 19, 22, 27; © Getty Images, pp. 11, 18; © Macduff Everton/CORBIS, p. 12; Illustration on p. 29 by Laura Westlund/Independent Picture Service.